Out of Body
A Practical Guide
Astral Plane
By Kensho

Copyright
All Information in this book is copyright to Kensho and Developed Life Books and may not be copied from, reproduced or sold without prior written permission.

Disclaimer
The information contained in this book is provided for general information and entertainment purposes only and does not constitute medical, psychiatric, legal or other professional advice on any subject matter. The author of this book does not accept any responsibility for any loss which may arise from reliance on information contained within this book or on any associated websites or blogs. The author of this book is NOT a licensed therapist and makes no claims to be. To read from here onward, it is assumed the reader has taken the diligence to read this message

KENSHO

The "Fire Lotus" Seal of Quality

The book you are about to read is a presentation by DevelopedLife.com. We pride ourselves on quality and hope that you find this information to be of great benefit.

Don't forget to visit the exclusive mailing list and Facebook group for Out of Body Travel by navigating to:

www.developedlife.com/kensho

This is where you can stay in contact with Kensho personally and further your education.

OUT OF BODY EXPERIENCES

Table of Contents

Prologue 6

Introduction 8

Chapter 1: Where it All Began 10

Chapter 2: The Different Dimensions 14

    Hells..17

Chapter 3: Common Misconceptions About Astral Travel....20

    Misconception 1: It's All in Your Brain....................20

    Misconception 2: It's a Sin 21

    Misconception 3: Shadow People Will Get You 21

    Misconception 4: You Can Die from Astral Traveling............22

    The Different Bodies of Existence 22

Chapter 4: The Difference Between Dreams, Lucid Dreaming, and Astral Projection 25

    But why do dreams happen and what's the difference with Astral Travel? 26

Chapter 5: Preparation for Astral Travel................30

    The Room..30

    The Mindset 31

    Duration..31

Chapter 6: O.B.E. Techniques 34

    The FARAON Mantram Technique............................34

    Sleep Paralysis 36

    The Process of Detaching your Astral Body from your Physical Body. 38

Chapter 7 : More OBE Techniques 42

    The LARASS Mantram Technique 42

    The EHIPTO Mantram Technique 42

    The RUSTY Mantram technique................................43

KENSHO

The Thai re re re re re Mantram technique 43

The Cricket Sound Technique 44

The Alarm Clock Technique 45

The Binaural/Theta Sound Techniques 45

Dream Masks 46

The future of dream masks 48

Apps 49

Chapter 8: The Magical Technique of the Angel's Trumpet .51

Chapter 9: Your First Steps in the Astral Dimension 55

Keeping yourself grounded to the astral 56

Astral Visibility 56

Traveling to places far away 57

My journeys into Egypt 58

Creating stuff in the astral. 60

Chapter 10: Lucid Dreaming Techniques 62

Evacuation 64

Inception 64

From Lucid to Pure Astral 66

Chapter 11: Meeting People While Out of Body 67

Mind Creations 67

Enlightened Beings 69

OBErs from the Physical 70

Temporary Astral Residents 74

Permanent Residents of the Astral 76

Setting up a collective practice 77

Chapter 12: Final Words 79

About the Author 81

More By Developed Life Books 83

OUT OF BODY EXPERIENCES

Ignorance is the curse of God; knowledge is the wing wherewith we fly to heaven.

William Shakespeare

Prologue

Dear reader: through the study and practice of this material, you will be able to achieve extraordinary and very enriching experiences, such as being awake in your dreams, interacting dynamically and creatively with your subconscious and even more interesting; creating new symbols and meanings within your transcendental universe.

Kensho, the author of this book is my friend and student, and he's been such for over 6 years, intensely practicing different techniques of astral projection, which I testify he knows and applies in his daily life.

Since I had the opportunity to reencounter him in this life, I knew he was going to be a very serious and dedicated student and during all these years he has shown me his sincere and deep interest in transcendental knowledge about the dream world.

With him, I have directed extraordinary practices such as; OBEs, detaching from the physical body, collective lucid dreams, remembrance and recapitulation of past lives, advanced meditations, and psycho-spiritual healings and revelations. For such reasons I encourage you, dear reader, to read and study this book that will open doors of extraordinary significance for your inner spiritual life and help your take advantage of the eight hours of sleep that ordinary people normally waste without ever getting to know all the potential they have in their own mind.

For more than 20 years I have been working closely with lucid dreams workshops and preparing people in the highest standards and levels of demand for them to transmit this knowledge to others.

I have studied and practiced with great teachers both Eastern and Western, which over the years have given me a heritage of experiences that have turned my life into a real treasure of knowledge and fulfillment.

Undoubtedly the direct experience of lucid dreaming and OBEs is something that will positively change your brain structure and give you more tools to lead your life through the transcendental path of awakening and human development.

OUT OF BODY EXPERIENCES

May applying this knowledge with a clear vision enrich your inner life and may your mind achieve the clear lucidity your soul needs. Lots of successes and happiness to you...

Om ah Hung
Dharmapa

Introduction

This book is an invitation to step into a world you've only heard through stories. This place is full of wonders reserved only to those who possess an open mind and are willing to step out from the multitude and see this reality through their own eyes. Once you experience this reality, you will never be the same, and perhaps with some luck, one day you will awaken to even greater potentials.

This world is called the Astral World, and you can discover this realm through a doorway called Astral Projection.

Astral Projection, also known as Out of Body Experiences (O.B.E.) is an experience that typically involves a sensation of being outside of one's body, looking at your unconscious physical body, moving around your immediate premises (like your bedroom), and experiencing otherworldly realms.

This phenomenon has intrigued humankind from ancient times and is abundant in the folklore, mythology, and spiritual narratives of most ancient and modern societies.

Through Astral Projection it is possible to experience a higher reality and travel to places that are inaccessible to the physical body. This means to visit other planets, to explore past lives, to go back in time, to witness historical events, to see dead relatives, to understand what happens when we die, to go to sacred temples that can't be seen in the physical world, to study and ask enlightened beings for guidance, to see the future, to go to sanctuaries of medicine and get cured of a disease, to meet people from long distances. The possibilities are limitless.

This book is written as a guide to have OBEs, it's based on my life's experiences, and is an educational tool as anyone can learn to have OBEs. I've been having them since the age of 15 and this has led me in a path of self-discovery in which I've studied different mystical traditions and with different spiritual masters. Needless to say, this has brought a lot of satisfaction to my life.

OUT OF BODY EXPERIENCES

I also intend to demystify the myths and fears surrounding Astral Projection that crop up time and again, but are based on ignorance.

Chapter 1: Where it All Began

When I was in primary school, my natural science book had a paragraph that read something like this:

Human life is made of the following stages:

1. *We are born*
2. *We grow up*
3. *We reproduce*
4. *We age*
5. *We die*

I had to memorize this over and over because I knew this question was going to show up in the exam, and the more I memorized it; the more boring and meaningless life seemed.

This created an impact on me. I could not settle with so little—I didn't want to be like the rest; there had to be more to life than this. I realize now why most people are unhappy with their lives, the educational system is designed to create machines, and they don't even question what is written in these books; they simply do what they're told: we are born, we grow up, we reproduce, we age, and we die. So sad how this is the destiny of most people.

I spent my childhood in a catholic school. The teachers and priest would always talk about God, heaven, and hell -- well, they mostly talked about hell -- but everything regarding creation and God was surrounded by mystery. I knew they just didn't know the answers I was looking for, for they were too scared to take a look at the unknown and find the answers for themselves.

Being a victim of bullying for a great part of my life, I amused myself with my imagination, thinking about other worlds, other possibilities, and escaping to a different reality. My usual reads were comic books, UFO magazines, and books about ghosts, psychic powers and other mysteries of the world. I have to confess that none of these reads directly influenced my interest on OBEs -- they talked about aliens, clairvoyance,

OUT OF BODY EXPERIENCES

telekinesis, etc. -- but the topic of astral projection was always missing.

My first interest on the subject came from my mother; she would tell me that when she was a little girl, she would lock herself in the bathroom, sit on the toilet seat and start repeating the phrase "I am I, I am I, I am I..." over and over again. She didn't know how she learned about that particular phrase, but what would happen next would be more intriguing; she described it as leaving her body and floating around the house being unseen by other people doing their normal day to day activities, and then coming back to her body.

Her younger sister also learned about this skill and would do exactly the same and get the same result. They were scared but thrilled about the experience and would repeat it often, until one day they told my grandmother and she told them that they shouldn't play with those things, as they were dangerous, and so they stopped doing it and lost interest. They never tried it or could even do it again, although my aunt would confirm about her childhood experiences when asked. My mother later lost any interest on topics that had to do with mysticism or the unexplained, however, it was interesting that she always referred to this experience as something that was not mere imagination from a child.

I tried to recreate this experience but never succeeded, I guess I also didn't put much effort into it, and since the topic was not discussed in any of my favorite reads, my interest soon faded, too. However, during this time I learned a skill that later proved to be helpful in the dream world: the ability to escape from nightmares. Whenever I was having a nightmare, it usually consisted of a monster chasing me to rip me apart. When the monster finally caught me, my heart was beating so fast that I would wake up drenched in sweat and I remained scared for the rest of day. As I became more focused on paying attention in my dreams, I learned that if I was having a nightmare the best thing I could do was to wake myself up, and so in my nightmares, I would concentrate on opening my eyes; I of course could see in the nightmare, but would do an extra effort to open my eyelids even more and this resulted in me actually opening my physical

KENSHO

eyelids which would result in waking up. I would use this ability often, and when I reached high school, nightmares then consisted of failing exams or being trapped inside the classroom; I would then use the same technique to escape every time.

One day, I had the most unusual experience: I was having a nightmare and applied my usual escaping technique, but when opening my eyes, I could see my room yet I could not move my body, the more I struggled, the less I could move; I was completely paralyzed. This scared me to death, after what seemed like many minutes of struggle, I finally seemed to lose consciousness, go back to dreaming and then I would wake up all of a sudden—finally able to move my body. I didn't associate this episode with having an OBE, and I even thought for a while that it was a demonic possession or something, and remained quite scared from the experience. This however, would repeat every few months or so, never lasting that long again, but scaring me nonetheless.

This continued happening for several years, until I reached college. One day studying in France as an exchange student, I was vacationing with my friends in the city of Avignon in the south of France and all four of us had to spend the night in a small room: Two guys and two girls. I was having a nightmare and decided to wake myself up as usual. Again, I could see the room but was paralyzed, and I started to call out for my friends to help, hoping they would try to wake me up. They didn't wake me up, however, they were able to hear me mumbling and one of them jokingly asked me if I was having an erotic dream. Feeling a bit ashamed, I decided to clarify the incident and told her about my experiences.

Surprisingly, she told me she would experience the same thing when sleeping facing up, and so that's why she would always sleep on a side to avoid this, and that she believed this is what people referred to as "astral travel". This term made an immediate impact on me. I had always wanted to astral travel but never really found a book that elaborated on the subject. Was I finally experiencing what my mother and aunt did when they were kids? I was soon to find out.

OUT OF BODY EXPERIENCES

Thanks to the magic of Internet, I immediately had access to many techniques on astral travel. Once I learned my first technique, I quickly put it into practice:

I first had a good workout session at the gym, came back home really tired, laid on my back pronouncing a mysterious mantra I had learned. I continued doing this until I started to feel sleepy, then I felt an electric sensation around my body. The next thing I knew I was floating in my room and could see a silver chord connected to my body lying still on the bed. I headed towards the window and could feel the cold glass and hear the sounds from the street. In my excitement I tried to go through the window but instead I was instantly pulled back to my physical body. I promptly woke up, stood up, and felt so happy because I thought I had achieved something great.

It was the beginning of a great journey, and the years to follow I had hundreds of experiences that changed my life. I even began teaching people how to astral project with great success and I hope this book helps you to be able to experience the astral world like I do.

Chapter 2: The Different Dimensions

In order to better understand the astral phenomenon, we have to talk about the different dimensions. This is a very useful subject for also trying to understand creation, religion, life after death, etc. But we're going to keep things simple and fast so that we can move on to the practical section of this book.

The Physical World: It is called the **third dimension**, because it is the base of the three dimensions and consists of length, height, and width. There are 48 different divine laws that control every physical object in this dimension. This includes laws of physics like gravity, and dimensional laws like distance. Understand that the more laws there are, the more restrictions there are, and thus the more suffering residents of that dimension will experience.

OUT OF BODY EXPERIENCES

The Vital World: This is the **fourth dimension**, real time has its base in this dimension. It is this dimension that missing objects and people often end up, such as with famous cases like the Bermuda Triangle. It is important to note that this is another **physical dimension** like ours, but it is a physical dimension with fewer laws (36 instead of 48). As a physical dimension, the correct way to explore it would be in your current physical body. This makes it more difficult to visit than the fifth dimension (astral) since your physical body is more adapted to the third dimension; and the fourth dimension would automatically reject and sort of "puke out" your current body. This fourth dimension can still be visited by using secret techniques called "Jinas" which are not covered in this book (perhaps the next one).

When the Mayans found out their civilization was going to meet the Spanish conquerors and be doomed, they transported many temples and people to the fourth dimension. Some of these temples became mountains in the third dimension, while the temples themselves and the people are invisible to us. Flying is possible there, so one could take the physical body up in the vital dimension, transport the physical body to great distances, and then finally return to the **third dimension**, in a totally different place. This would actually be known as tele-transportation. There's a movie that sort of talks about Jinas tele-transportation (Jumper, 2008).

In summary, ancient civilizations, intraterrestrials, temples, and masters all live happily in this higher physical dimension.

Next, **The Astral World and The Mental World** are the **fifth dimension** which is divided by lower and higher spheres. The lower part is the astral world, and the higher part is the mental world. We normally visit the lower part of the astral world every night when we go to sleep, and we do so with a special body called **The Astral Body**. This is our primary vessel we use when we astral project, and it's the body the residents of the astral plane use.

There are 24 laws in this dimension. Gravity, time, distance, and other laws do not exist there, therefore it is

KENSHO

possible to go anywhere, and anytime, as quick as one can think. Masters, temples and other higher beings also reside in this dimension. Even though we visit this plane every time we go to sleep, we don't even realize it because our perception is completely distracted by dream imagery produced by the mind. This imaginary blinds us from seeing the real astral world; and our lack of practice, concentration and awareness makes us forget many parts of our dreams as well as interactions with the astral world.

Thus the fifth dimension is the dimension when dreams also take place and it is also the dimension people normally go to when they die. The more aware (the less karma) a person has in life makes that person more aware of the fifth dimension when he passes away, and the more aware that person is the more that person has the power to explore, interact and be aware of his or her existence in this higher state. This is what we normally refer as "going to heaven".

And the more asleep a person is in life (consciously, spiritually unaware and possessing high amounts of karma from negative actions) makes that person more asleep in the astral dimension when he passes away. This could lead to negative conditions in the astral, whereupon the he or she is living in his/her own nightmares and negative memories, which could be close to what we normally think of "going to hell" is like. (Note: there are other, more specific planes that could be considered to be real hells and heavens—but this topic is beyond the scope of this book.)

Next is the **Sixth Dimension**, which is divided between the Buddhic world and The Causal world. This dimension and the Seventh represent the "real" heaven that spiritual teachers through the ages aspire to enter.

One can experience a glimpse of these higher worlds through meditation. Some people describe these meditation experiences as "losing the ego" or "sense of self" and "fusing with everything", etc.

Finally, we come to **The Atmic World**, or the **seventh dimension** which is the home of our inner being; that divine spark which is part of God. In other words, God lives in this dimension. These last two dimensions are hard to describe since they are worlds in which we use superior bodies of our intimate selves.

Keep in mind that life in higher planes is usually only temporary, since most people have to eventually come back to physical worlds in order to work on eliminating karma (negative action that causes negative reaction), and karma is also related to the level of awareness a person has. Once the person has eliminated his karma in the physical world, it also means that the person has awakened a higher awareness which would make that person able to stop being limited by the perception of being bound to a physical body living in a physical world, and so his learning journey in the physical world would be complete, and he would now be ready to start another learning process in the astral world, and so on—getting closer to God little by little, evolving, and living in the different heavens. This is what religions have been trying to teach us all this time. As you can see, life is a constant evolution for the soul.

By astral traveling, a person can start experiencing higher dimensions, different realities, and different possibilities. A problem we face today is that people are unaware of the existence of higher dimensions; when life in the physical world is bad then there's much suffering because that person believes there are no other possibilities. People are so afraid of death that when a person dies, we weep. People say they believe in heaven (which is just a higher dimension) yet are afraid of seeing this reality with their own eyes. They could overcome fear if they could find out what awaits them in the afterlife!

As complicated as all of this might sound, everything becomes clear once a person learns to venture into the astral world.

Hells

Hells are the infra dimensions that are lower than the 3rd dimension or physical world. This is why the physical world is described as being "in the middle of heaven and hell". It is the division line.

The contrast between a hell and lighter, heavenly realms is that as one moves to higher planes, they become freer and less constrained by laws—however, as one moves to lower realms then one is more restricted and suffocated by additional laws that we do not even deal with on Earth. The first hell has 96 laws (that's double that of the 48 laws of the physical world) and the next hell has 192 laws, etc.

To help you to understand this concept, think for a moment about some of the laws of the physical world: drinking water, eating, breathing to sustain oneself, etc. And then, on top of this we make our lives more miserable by creating passports, taxes, etc. In a higher, heavenly dimension such as the astral, one can feed from the astral light as the sole source of sustenance, no need for water or food as requirements to survive. As a result, we experience greater freedom to express ourselves without being confined by what we call the day-to-day routine.

Now imagine a lower dimension such as a hell, the amount of additional laws to live by creates indescribable suffering.

Fortunately, it's important to note that going to hell isn't an easy thing, as one must have been really asleep and miserable, creating a lot of karma through many existences in the physical world in order to start gaining access to hell. For example, a person who may be bound to a hellish dimension may first start living a type of hell on earth; such as a terminal drug addict unable to break free from his addiction and is a slave of his vice, or a person with deteriorating health, living in a terrible situation on the street and attracting individuals, energies and events related to that hellish state of being. When experiencing physical death, then such a person's consciousness would continue living in an infra-dimension related to the psychological state of being he had before dying.

Religions try to teach the techniques to liberate oneself from the attachment and veil of illusion in the physical world, thereby saving oneself from hell in the process. And, because our plane exists in-between heaven and hell, we humans experience

OUT OF BODY EXPERIENCES

many good moments as well as bad moments. In reality most of mankind suffers a lot, and these bad moments take the most precedence. The message that great Masters have tried to communicate to us is that we can evolve and free ourselves from the suffering we experience in this world and stop coming back to the cycle of rebirth in the physical world. If we can end this cycle we can then continue our evolutionary path into greater dimensions.

Since "seeing is believing", then experiencing the astral world would help us to expand our comprehension of the meaning of life. Experimenting first hand would help us to free our minds, expand our consciousness, and discover the possibilities of life beyond the physical world, which can feel very liberating.

Chapter 3: Common Misconceptions About Astral Travel

When I bring the subject of astral travel to the conversation, the first thing that comes to mind for a lot of people is: "That's dangerous, you could die. It's like playing with fire. Your soul could get lost. Your physical body can get 'snatched' by a ghost or demon."

There are even new horror movies that deal with the subject in a negative light, such as the movie *Insidious*.

It's important that you understand that these beliefs are false, since they can totally ruin your astral experience or ability to astral travel forever. There's a close relation between beliefs, the mind, and the astral.

Believing that astral travel is dangerous can totally block your ability to astral project. Filling your mind with fear can create frightening mind-projections in your dreams and the astral. Watching too many horror films can bring horror scenes directly to your dreams or astral travels. In the Astral World, the mind has the ability to create things from the ether. In other words, your thoughts become creations.

This is actually true for the physical world as well, except that thoughts take more time to materialize in the physical world (this is related to the law of attraction which is beyond the scope of this book).

Before we go too much further in this book, I feel it's important to first list a few of the reservations and insecurities like this which may prevent a new astral explorer from fully developing the skill.

Misconception 1: It's All in Your Brain

OUT OF BODY EXPERIENCES

Some feel the whole experience is subjective (not real) and part of a dream like phenomenon, therefore astral projection is a waste of time. As we'll discuss later, sometimes there is a mix of subjective phenomena (dream creations) that usually arise out of the lucid dreaming state rather than the astral state. However, this is just one part of it, as during a true visit to the astral plane you will experience real (objective) people (other astral travelers, Masters, residents of the astral planes, and so forth). It's important to point out that astral projection is not lucid dreaming, and people who have done both have no problems recognizing the difference.

As I will talk about later in this book, there are also personal experiences that can occur which quickly remove a skeptic's doubts. As you learn this skill, it is likely some of these experiences will eventually happen to you, as well.

Misconception 2: It's a Sin

Many religious people seem to be afraid of astral projection and claim that it is condemned in scripture, the Bible, the Qu'ran, etc. As I talk about before, making a direct link with the higher dimensions allows a person to understand the reality behind what lessons scriptures and holy books are trying to teach. Separating from your physical body is also a natural thing that everybody does at night, even if one is not aware of it. By this definition, since everyone can (and does) leave their bodies, everyone would therefore be a sinner!

Misconception 3: Shadow People Will Get You

There are some who believe creatures lurk in the astral and will get you. Firstly, no creature can actually harm your astral body as it is made of energy, which is indestructible. Secondly, while some people have negative experiences that they talk about on the internet, it doesn't apply for everyone. As I've said already, our thoughts can create the reality around us (or at the very least—convincing dream illusions), and maybe some people, because they are full of fear, will project an idea from a horror movie that's stuck in their minds, and then mistakenly believe the astral realm has some evil creature living inside of it. However, as I'll talk about later, dream projections are just a part of your own mind, and can be very easily dismissed / made to go away. If anything, it's just a lesson to remove garbage and negative thoughts from your mind.

Misconception 4: You Can Die from Astral Traveling

Some people think that having an astral travel experience can potentially kill you since "your soul leaves your body, and might not come back."

First of all, it's important to clarify that when you astral project, your soul is not leaving your body. The human soul is beyond the barrier of existence of the physical body. The soul is your divine spark, the part of you that is part of God, your bond with God, and this spark manifests through your different bodies and through different dimensions. It's impossible to lose your soul.

What actually leaves your body through astral travel, is your astral body. The astral body is one of multiple bodies of your existence, which allow you to experience reality through different dimensions. These bodies are connected yet independent.

As we have already spoken about the different dimensions, now would be a good point to actually talk about the different bodies we possess.

The Different Bodies of Existence

1. **Physical Body**: I guess there's no need for explanation as to what a physical body is, except to clarify that your physical body is your vehicle for the third dimension.

2. **Vital or Etheric Body**: This is the aura that surrounds the physical body and which can be perceived by certain

OUT OF BODY EXPERIENCES

individuals or after developing certain skills. The Etheric Body is a body of energy that gives 'the spark of life' to all living creatures. When the Etheric Body gets sick — either by natural diseases or problems of the mind (such as stress) — then the physical body gets sick. The Vital or Etheric Body is tied to the physical dimension along with the physical body.

3. **Astral Body**: Your vehicle for the 5th dimension. It has a subtler composition for a subtler dimension. For this reason, the astral body can pass through objects that are in the physical world, levitate, expand, shrink, travel instantly, and change by will. It belongs to the 5th dimension, also known as the Astral, with far fewer laws that can constrict it (24). Although the astral body is subtle, when it interacts with other astral matter it's still perfectly solid (for instance, running your fingers through the dirt in an astral forest).

When you dream, you're already experiencing the Astral Dimension, except that your awareness is greatly diminished and you are unable to fully perceive the reality of the Astral around you.

4. **Mental Body**: Your vehicle for the 5th superior dimension. The Astral World is the 5th inferior, while the Mental World is the 5th superior. This world is related to the mind, and is sometimes known as the Higher Astral. Your body becomes even more subtle and fluid in this world.

There are another 3 bodies that compose the human existence, as well. However, their explanation is beyond the scope of this book, and will be saved for more advanced studies later.

The Silver Cord

Finally, we cannot forget that the Astral Body is connected to the physical body through a silver cord. When a person dies, the silver cord gets severed. The physical body is then discarded and the person acquires a degree of awareness of the 5th dimension.

KENSHO

The higher the level of awareness the person had in the physical dimension, the higher awareness he gets of the 5th dimension after death. In other words, people who live infatuated by material life, being victims of their passions, money and possessions, or emotional/psychological dramas and who lack spirituality, one day die and believe they're still living in the physical world. Then, their mind starts recreating all of these scenes in the Astral Plane, even their last moments of disease and death. Little by little, the person starts realizing that he or she has passed away and becomes familiarized with the Astral Plane as one's new home and can begin to enjoy life in this higher plane of existence. The higher the person's awareness was in physical life, the faster that person recognizes and embraces life in the true astral world.

The silver cord will only be severed when the person's time on earth has reached an end according to that person's *karma* (action and reaction), and other divine laws that come into play. In other words, the silver cord gets severed and the person physically dies *only when that person has to*, and it can't be influenced just by going on an astral excursion.

So as you can see, we never really die, we simply change bodies and awareness of our reality. Truly René Descartes' philosophical proposition "I think, therefore I am" gets new attention: Having a physical body does not make you alive, being aware does.

Chapter 4: The Difference Between Dreams, Lucid Dreaming, and Astral Projection

During the day, our body experiences hundreds if not thousands of sensations: visual stimuli, smells, sounds, feel, taste, temperature, etc. It is during this time that our brain is tuned with certain types of brain-wave frequencies known as the **beta brain waves**.

Beta brain waves are associated with normal waking consciousness and a heightened state of alertness, logic and critical reasoning.

When we start the process of sleeping we go through different **sleep stages**:

1) **Alpha**: Our body starts relaxing, this is known as the stage of Alpha brain waves, light meditation also induces this Alpha brain wave activity and is really relaxing.

2) **Theta:** we then go into a different stage of brain activity in which out body gets "shut down" from most sensations, this is known as the **Theta brain wave state**, and this allows our awareness to stop being identified so much with the physical body to the point where it could then focus on the Astral Body as its shell/vehicle. in other words, it is the perfect stage for having OBEs. This stage is also achieved under deep meditation and through it we can actually establish a mental connection with higher dimensions and our higher self. Sadly, most of us are not used to experiencing this stage of brain activity for long and we quickly fall into the next stage.

3) **Delta**. The Delta brain wave stage is when we lose complete awareness, it is when we simply "black out" and this lasts some 30 minutes. The Delta ruins everything for us when we want to be conscious of have an OBE, and this happens to most people every night.

After the Delta stage our brain enters again into the Theta and Alpha stages of brain wave activity and the Astral Body detaches itself from the physical body and roams free in the 5th dimension, however we normally don't notice this because after the "blackout" caused from the Delta stage our brain has a hard time regaining awareness. We eventually gain a form of minimum awareness, but this is not enough to realize what is happening, and because of this we usually just start dreaming. Many people also tend to forget their dreams and simply believe they didn't dream at all.

So in other words, your Astral Body leaves your physical body every time you sleep and after all this time you probably haven't even noticed. However, our ability to maintain awareness can be severely damaged by our physical brain that is shooting interfering (delta) waves into us, as well as our general lack of awareness and practice of becoming aware of the astral (see below):

But why do dreams happen and what's the difference with Astral Travel?

Dreams happen because the person is not even half aware during the dream, just like people are not 100% aware during day time. If they were, we would be surrounded by geniuses. And because of this lack of awareness, the person starts 'projecting' memories and thoughts into the Astral World or 5th dimension. Since the person is not very aware then he cannot control these projections and becomes identified/infatuated with them, following along these illusions to nowhere.

So the person basically creates some sort of 'illusion shield' around him that prevents that person from observing the real Astral World.

I like to describe this as wearing a virtual reality visor that is displaying memories and thoughts the person follows along without perceiving that he might actually be, for example, in a beautiful forest of the Astral World, and if that person could take that visor away then that he could actually see that beautiful astral forest.

I've been in many situations in the Astral where I've seen people walking around in their astral bodies with a blank stare, mumbling words and repeating every day actions such as working, very similar to people who sleep walk. In some occasions I approached them and told them they were dreaming to see if I could get them to become aware in the Astral but somehow they couldn't listen to me and remained dreaming.

It is of course much better and productive to achieve Astral Travel instead of dreaming, but dreams shouldn't be seen as mere useless fabrications of the mind since they also contain a specific language and internal messages coming from the repressed desires of our subconscious mind to which we can listen to and then try to turn to reality in the physical world. During dreams we also receive messages from the "supraconsciousness", that higher self within us, that universal mind to which we're connected to that can give us important messages or signs for our evolutionary development. It's for this reason that we must keep a dream diary. I highly recommend studying the work of Carl Jung, as it can help to understand the symbolism in dreams.

Some dreams are prophetic in nature too, and it's an incredible sensation when you go back to your diary to see that you had indeed written down the prophetic dream some time before it occurred. I remember I once dreamed that I was riding a bike with a friend in a busy American street and we were having so much fun. Then a month later, the friend from the dream, who was living in another city came to visit me, and he suggested we rent some bikes to go biking in downtown San Diego. We did, and suddenly all the images from the dream started happening before me, and I told him about the dream and at the end of the day I was able to show him what I had written in the diary, and he was astounded from the accuracy. This is only one of many prophetic dreams I've had in my life.

So as we mentioned before, Astral Travel then, is basically to take away that dream illusion and perceive the Astral World the way it is in its pure form, without illusions or fabrications from the mind, without dream imaginary. This can be achieved in two ways that I will explain now: *Astral Projection and Lucid Dreaming.*

Astral Projection

Astral Projection is when a person goes to bed and consciously starts performing certain techniques to avoid the "blackout" and ensuing dream-state in order to have a direct experience of the Astral World through an OBE.

By doing this correctly the person feels that the physical body has become asleep and unresponsive while the mind is still conscious. By stopping the constant stimuli from the physical body, the mind can easily detach the astral body from the physical body; at which point your mind will immediately be experiencing the astral dimension.

As we mentioned earlier, the process of detaching the Astral Body from the Physical Body happens every night when the person falls asleep but the person is always unaware of this phenomenon because he has lost consciousness, and even when that person regains some sort of consciousness--this consciousness is very limited, confused, and focused in the dream, even though this person is really operating out of the astral.

OUT OF BODY EXPERIENCES

Lucid Dreaming

Lucid Dreaming on the other hand, happens when the person has already lost consciousness, starts dreaming, but then with the use of specific techniques practiced during the day, the person realizes that he is sleeping and stops following the dream imaginary/creations of his own mind and starts exploring the Astral World instead.

Normally in this situation the Astral World retains some dream imaginary, thus the person is not as aware and the Astral World is not as "clear" as in Astral Projection, but the person can still explore and experience the Astral World greatly, especially as the dream state melts away.

The person can also consciously interact with the dream imaginary and dream characters and obtain certain information, as they contain knowledge from the person's subconscious as well as superconscious mind. Lucid dreams have thus many degrees of "clarity" all depending on how aware that person is while having them.

So without further-ado let us now go to the practical part of the book.

Chapter 5: Preparation for Astral Travel

The most important part of astral projection is to have the right mindset. If you're constantly nervous, fearing the unknown, being negative, etc. then it will be really hard for you to astral travel.

In fact, the word "hard" should be deleted from your vocabulary. Astral travel is mostly directed by the mind. By Astral traveling and exploring the dream world you will realize how fast your thoughts become a reality in these planes, therefore you should start training the mind to increase your chances of successfully astral traveling.

The Room

You must make an effort to keep your room clean and tidy. Messy rooms bring heavy negative energies, keep your room smelling good, I suggest using incenses and aromatic oils or aromatic candles.

Turn your room into your own very magical shrine if you will.

If possible, try to have your bed pointing north (your head pointing north when you sleep, that is) this greatly increases your chances to go out of body. If this is not possible, then try to aim it eastward.

Sound is important, I don't recommend listening to a lot of hard rock or heavy metal. Listening to classical or relaxation music before going to sleep is a good idea.

Also avoid watching TV at least 1 hour before going to bed as the images will be fresh and imprinted on your mind.

Always sleep on your back with your face facing the ceiling. The best hour to sleep is between 9:30 – 10:00 p.m. It gets your body and mind in synchronicity with the night cycle, and by attuning with the vibrations and cycles of nature you will maximize your chances. However if you can't follow this night time don't let that prevent you from trying; we understand that everybody has different busy schedules that can't be compromised.

Have a very light dinner at least an hour or more before going to bed.

The Mindset

You should never think about anything bad or negative happening to you.

When laying on your back tell yourself "I'm going to Astral Travel", train your mind with that affirmation.

Make sure you are free of mental clutter. Astral travel is not a time to be obsessing or ruminating about fears, anxieties, and daily worries. All of this will interfere with your ability to leave your body, and could even lead to a negative experience.

Some simple breathing exercises and meditative practices for relaxation are a good idea. Take some time before beginning to perhaps light your incense or perform other routines that will help you to focus on the moment and be less concerned with what happened to you throughout the day. Do not go on Facebook or YouTube or else your mind will become preoccupied with that stimuli, and it will interfere with your ability to go out of body.

Duration

The duration before an OBE occurs will depend entirely on the willingness of the person. If you are not achieving the OBE and can't sleep either, but don't have to go to work or school the next day or otherwise don't care about sleep quality, then don't stop using the techniques (outlined soon) as long as you remain in bed. There've been times when I didn't have anything to do the next day and wasn't sleepy either—which are the perfect conditions to try the technique until 7 am in the morning. Around this time I finally started feeling sleepy, which meant

KENSHO

having to fight to not fall asleep by continuing doing the technique. Then, finally after a whole night of work, I'll have achieved the OBE. To me, for some reason, feeling unable to sleep until finally feeling sleepy late in the morning works great to achieve an OBE.

Also you must practice each of the techniques I am about to present for at least 2 weeks each, don't mix techniques during the same night.

Hey! You Reading This – Slow Down a Sec! There's Something You Need to Know:

Kensho, along with *Developed Life Magazine*, are putting together a community for astral travelers. This includes a mailing list and a Facebook group for people who want to learn more and meet others interested in this subject.

You can get started by following this link: www.developedlife.com/kensho. We hope to see you there!

Chapter 6: O.B.E. Techniques

After following the preparation advice and laying on your back, close your eyes, then proceed to say this phrase: "Divine mother, please help me to have an astral travel experience". "Divine father, please help me to astral travel". Note: We'll talk more about why we are mentioning the Divine Mother or Divine Father later, in chapter 11. Then, proceed to use a technique, such as:

The FARAON Mantram Technique

A **Mantram** is a word whose sounds activate the Chakras (energy points) in the body. Mantrams for O.B.E. activate the specific Chakras that will help the person to leave theirbody.
The person takes a breath and pronounces

Fffffaaaaaaaaaaa
[takes a breath]
Rrrrrrraaaaaaaa
[takes a breath]
Ooooonnnn

Take a breath and starts over again with Fffffaaaaaaaaaaa and so on...
Depending on how tired you are you will feel sleepy and the mantram will become hard to pronounce, this is ok and desirable.
The person can also choose to say the mantram verbally at the beginning and then switch to doing it mentally (especially if the person is not feeling tired) or to do it mentally right from the beginning. This is all acceptable though doing it verbally could have greater effect and prevent yourself from falling asleep.

OUT OF BODY EXPERIENCES

If done correctly and with practice, the person's body will fall asleep but the person's mind will remain awake. The person might experience any or all of the following:

- A tingling sensation in the body
- A feeling of electricity running through the body
- Hearing weird sounds
- Unable to move the body
- Feel the body light or heavy or actually feel as if somebody is sitting on top of him.

The last one is important because many people describe it as a ghost or demon sitting on top of them which can be terrifying, but in reality it has to do with the changes and effects the Astral body upon the physical during the phase of it's natural detachment from the physical body. As we have stated before, it is something that happens every time we sleep, but this time our perception is awake and attentive from the beginning.

A very early depiction of the belief of a demon or goblin sitting on top of your body. In reality it's just the physical effects of your astral body disconnecting.

It is therefore important to make a pause here and shift to the topic of sleep paralysis.

Sleep Paralysis

A phenomenon that is experienced by a lot of people at sleep time and that scares them deeply is sleep paralysis. When this happens, the person describes being unable to move his/her physical body and sometimes hears noises or feels the weight phenomenon we just discussed pressing down on top of him or her.

We fear what we don't understand and unfortunately, having these experiences without a clear understanding makes people want to avoid them at all costs. Most who experience early stages of the OBE are completely unaware of the fact that because they could feel the sleep paralysis, they were very close to entering the astral dimension, and that it was nothing to be afraid of. Understand that any fear of experimenting with these phenomena will block you from having OBEs.

For this reason in this chapter we'll explain how to deal with sleep paralysis.

Some theories state that sleep paralysis results from disrupted REM sleep, which normally induces complete muscle atonia (muscle weakness) to prevent the sleeper from acting out his or her dreams (I once broke a night table and almost broke my foot by acting out a dream, so I guess sleep paralysis is a very useful phenomenon).

Whatever the reason why sleep paralysis happens we must learn to use it to our advantage because being unable to move/feel the physical body is an excellent tool to experience the world out of our physical body. It is during sleep paralysis when we can easily induce an OBE.

So always keep these 3 rules during sleep paralysis:

1. Keep Calm

OUT OF BODY EXPERIENCES

Struggling will only bring more anxiety which will give a negative tone to the experience and will take you out of the right mindset. **When you are in sleep paralysis you should focus on doing the mantralization mentally that we discussed before, or any other technique you were using for achieving the OBE.**

2. Don't Fear

Nothing bad can happen to you during this time. You always go through this stage of paralysis but are always unconscious and don't notice it. Every morning you wake up unscratched/unspoiled and if you are reading this book then you're not dead nor will sleep paralysis be a cause of death.
    The mind is very strong in the astral dimension, so thoughts will become reality. This is why the mind can be both very helpful here but it can also be a negative influence. That's why we must learn to control it since all your fears will become "real" or at least visibly manifested somehow in the astral.
    After many years of having OBEs I've realized that what most people describe as ghosts or demons are nothing but creations of the mind. I remember one day I watched a horror movie called "Mama", about two girls who lost their mother, who later comes back as a ghost. The movie was quite scary and I watched it in the middle of the night, so when I went to bed I had

the image of the ghost imprinted on my mind. That night I was able to have an OBE and what was the first thing I saw? Mama!

However, during this OBE I knew that my mind had created the image of this monster and the monster itself was just there doing nothing, a mind creation just waiting for my further input. If I had lost control of my mind and feared being attacked by Mama then Mama would have gone straight at me in an attacking course, but it just stood there with no programming of its own. However the look of it just became too annoying for me to continue having the OBE and I couldn't stay in the astral for long.

This was an interesting experience nevertheless, as it showed me how powerful our minds are. We will discuss in another chapter how to use our imagination to create things in the astral dimension.

3. Don't waste your time

If you've experienced sleep paralysis in the past then you would know one thing: it doesn't happen very often.

Which also means that being aware of your body being asleep, and the transition to the astral dimension, are not exactly things you experience in your day to day. It is for this very reason that you must **embrace** and try to profit from this experience. We'll now discuss the procedure to achieve this transition.

The Process of Detaching your Astral Body from your Physical Body.

So you were doing your practice to induce an OBE and you find yourself lying on your bed experiencing all sorts of things. You might have experienced a tingling sensation on your body, you might or might have not heard weird noises or felt weights sitting on top of you and perhaps now you feel like you can't move your physical body. Congratulations, you're all set!

OUT OF BODY EXPERIENCES

Notice that most of the time when feeling the sleep paralysis people can actually see their room, bed and body just as if they had their eyes open at night, although as we mentioned earlier in the preparation procedure, you actually closed your eyes. In fact, your eyes are closed but you are seeing things through your astral eyes without even realizing it at the moment.

It is now that you can try the following techniques to detach your astral body from your physical body. Keep in mind, as we've mentioned previously that your astral body **always** detaches itself from your physical body when you go to sleep and it is also true that although the astral body detaches itself from the physical body, it is always connected to it through the use of the silver cord; a powerful "destiny cord" that cannot be cut by anyone but the angels of death when it is your time to transition. The only difference when your astral body leaves on this occasion is that you are aware of it, and because of that, it might just shy away from completing the task.

Note that you shouldn't take anything in this book as an absolute since everybody is different, what works for some might not work for others. There are people who find it natural and easy to leave their physical body after experiencing some sleep paralysis, others might find it more difficult. Also you shouldn't train your mind to believe there's only one way of doing things, you might come up with your own techniques, etc.

What we're going to list here are just some techniques to make the process of leaving your physical body with your astral body easier, and these techniques are based on teachings I've received, things I've learned and feedback from people's experiences. Choose any or all of these techniques as best suits you:

1. Getting up from bed

The simplest technique is to get up from bed the way you normally do with your physical body, except that this time you will do so focusing on your astral body. When you are experiencing sleeping paralysis, relax, keep doing your astral technique mentally and do the exact same movements you normally do to get up from bed but without forcing it, without applying much effort. You can count to three and then roll to the side of bed you normally get up from and do it. If it fails, relax, count to three and try again. Sometimes you might even feel as part of you detached from your physical body but some other parts didn't and you feel like getting dragged back to your physical body. That's ok, just keep trying, you almost got it.

2. The Ghost Hand Technique

When you are experiencing sleeping paralysis, relax, keep doing your astral technique mentally and imagining you are detaching **your ghostly hands,** i.e.,imagine your astral body as a translucent sheath that covers your body like an outer layer of the same shape as your body, in other words, like a ghostly figure of you. And what you want to do is to first detach these ghostly astral hands. Don't do this with much physical effort nor with abrupt movements or that will wake you up, just use mainly your imagination and once you actually see these ghostly hands detaching from your physical body put them up front where you can see them.

Now that you can see your astral hands, proceed to try to get up from bed with this ghostly astral body using the same movements you normally use when getting up from bed with your physical body, except that this time you will do it softly and focusing on doing so with your astral body.

That's it, that's the way this technique works!

3. The rolling technique

In sleep paralysis, relax, then roll your astral body on one side of the bed as many times as to be ejected from the bed and into freedom.

4. The rope technique

OUT OF BODY EXPERIENCES

Imagine there's a rope hanging on top of you, either visible or invisible. Imagine you grab it with your astral hands and start pulling your astral body up until you leave your physical body.

5. The teleportation technique

This is the technique I mostly use nowadays. When feeling the transition effects on your body or at sleep paralysis, imagine being teleported to a place inside the room, this place could be, for example, a few feet next to your bed, since you are familiarized with your surroundings then this visualization should be easy. Just feel like being there, seeing from there, and you will be teleported there with your astral body.

These were just some basic detachment techniques, you might as well come up with the ones of your own.

Once you get up from bed with your astral body, remain calm You can stare at your physical body if you like, but this is not recommended as thinking on your physical body will drag you back to it. In fact, you will soon learn how staying in the astral requires lots of concentration. Don't worry about not coming back, because you'll soon learn it's hard to not return.

If you do stare at your physical body you might either see your physical body sleeping, you might see the silver cord leading to it or you might actually not find your physical body, which is also something normal as now you are in a different dimension and sometimes you will be able to see things in the physical world and sometimes you will not. (Although the surroundings look familiar, these are just the physical impressions upon this part of the astral plane closest to the earth plane).

You might also see the astral equivalent of things, persons, animals and places. Sometimes a place you know well in the physical could be completely different in the astral.

Chapter 7 : More OBE Techniques

Now that you understand the basics, let's explore more methods to get out of your body.

The LARASS Mantram Technique

The person takes a breath and pronounces
Lllllllaaaaaaaaaaaa
[takes a breath]
Rrrrrrraaaaaaaaa
[takes a breath]
Sssssssssssssssssss

Take a breath and starts over again with Lllllaaaaaaaaaa and so on...

Depending on how tired you are you will feel sleepy, and the mantram will become hard to pronounce. This is ok and desirable.

The person can also choose to say the mantram verbally at the beginning and then switch to do it mentally (especially if the person is not feeling tired) or to do it mentally right from the beginning, this is all acceptable though doing it verbally could have greater effect.

If done correctly and with practice, the person's body will fall asleep but the person's mind will remain awake.

The EHIPTO Mantram Technique

The person takes a breath and pronounces
Eeeeeeeeeeeeeeehhh (the eeee.... sounds like eh)
[takes a breath]

OUT OF BODY EXPERIENCES

Hhiiiiiiiiiiiiiiiiiiiiiiippppppppp (iiiiiii.... sounds like ee, the whole thing is a long "hip" sound so don't forget to pronounce the "h" as well)
[takes a breath]
Tttoooooooooooooooooooo (oooo... sounds like oh)
Take a breath and start over again with Eeeeeeeeeeeh and so on...

The RUSTY Mantram technique

The person takes a breath and pronounces
Rrrruuuuuuuuuuuu
[takes a breath]
Sssssssssssssssssssssssssssss
[takes a breath]
Tyyyyyyyyyyyyyyyyyyyyyy (the yyy.... sounds like ee)
Take a breath and start over again with Rrrruuuuuuuuuuuu and so on...

The Thai re re re re re Mantram technique

The person takes a breath and pronounces
Tttthhaaaaaaaiiiii
[takes a breath]
Re re re re re (The 'r' is a soft r)
[takes a breath]
Tttthhaaaaaaaiiiii
[takes a breath]
Re re re re re
Take a breath and starts over again with Ttthhaaaaaiiiiii and so on...

The Cricket Sound Technique

This technique consists of searching for the cricket sound inside of your head. You've probably heard this cricket-like sound inside your head sometimes in your life, it is similar to the sound you hear when you leave an old TV on without signal or turned on but on 'mute'. Some appliances also make this subtle vibrational sound when in stand-by.

Once you hear this cricket-like sound inside your head, concentrate on it, the more you do the clearer it will sound.

Do this when lying in bed ready to go to sleep and facing up, it will have a similar effect to the mantrams, so follow the procedure.

One can boost this technique by hearing the sound of a real cricket at night or a recording, then one will notice that this sound resounds inside your head. This is the pineal gland being stimulated through concentration.

This is the reason why crickets represent the voice of consciousness in many cultures and religions, remember Jiminy Cricket from Pinocchio?

Aztec Cricket symbol outside Chapultepec, Mexico

The Alarm Clock Technique

This technique consists of setting up an alarm clock to start ringing many times at night, which will undoubtedly wake you up to turn off the alarm, and it will leave you tired and sleepy since this is not your normal waking hour; and if you're working with the idea of having an OBE then you will go back to sleep using one of the other techniques such as Mantrams. Since you're tired then your body will have no problem relaxing and sleeping while your mind will hopefully remain awake as you follow a Mantram. The alarm can be setup many times at night in order to maximize your chances.

The Binaural/Theta Sound Techniques

This technique is very interesting because of the obvious vibrations you will feel in your body. Get yourself an MP3 player, iPhone, CD player, etc. and a good pair of comfortable headphones (the comfort part is very important), alternatively you can also use speakers.

Now, download any binaural beat/song for Astral Projection and listen to it. These songs can be found all over the internet, especially in YouTube by searching for the keywords: astral projection, binaural, song, sound. There are also websites if you Google them which allow you to convert YouTube videos into Mp3s.

You will feel a tingling sensation in your body, this can progressively increase. As you feel the tingling, perform the other out of body techniques or Mantrams.

An expert astral traveler can have an OBE during the day with this technique but the beginner will perhaps need other considerations to achieve it; some drowsiness/sleepiness is needed, also the practitioner can drink one or two glasses of wine to help relax.

Perhaps you have tried this technique before without success but this perhaps had to do with the fact you lacked the other advices from this book (what to do during sleep paralysis, astral body detaching techniques, etc.). So if you put everything together I guarantee the results will be highly positive.

Dream Masks

Now this is something worth trying! Dream masks, also known as Lucid Dreaming Masks (Google them) are basically sleep masks that you put on when going to sleep which have incorporated technologies in the form of visual or auditory signals in order to induce Astral Projection or Lucid Dreams. They work similarly to reality checks (a lucid dreaming technique I'll discuss in a later chapter).

I've tried many of them and I can tell you they are great aids for achieving OBEs.

The most popular and basic designs out there consist of a sleeping mask with light diodes (old LED-like lights) at eye level and an incorporated timer. Once the mask is turned on then the light diodes will start flashing after 45 -60 minutes, and will flash for a few seconds after some intervals.

The idea is to have the mask on as you begin dreaming. As you are dreaming you will suddenly see the dream world turning red (the color of the light diodes) or see strong flashes of red light, or even an ambulance approaching. At that moment you pause within your dream and ask yourself "what the heck?" and that's when you figure out you are dreaming, that you have the mask on, and you become lucid, which will allow you to start exploring the dream consciously, and then transition into astral projection (as discussed before through the lucid dreaming method).

Alternatively the red flashes could wake you up suddenly, though you're still tired and sleepy and this can leave you in a state of quickly going back to sleep but with a fresher awareness. Or being woken up lightly will put you in a state of sleep paralysis in which case you know the techniques to use this state to your advantage and detach yourself from your physical body.

45 – 60 minutes after going to bed is thought to be the time where most people are going through the Theta state and

OUT OF BODY EXPERIENCES

having REM (Rapid Eye Movements), as we mentioned before this is the perfect state for achieving an OBE and so dream masks are programmed to activate at this time.

In my opinion, these masks were really effective but they did have their drawbacks, especially on long term usage. The main problem was that they were not comfortable, they were a bit heavy and sometimes you could even feel the parts, nothing like a regular sleep mask, so sometimes it was hard to feel comfortable enough to actually fall asleep, and I'd end up fed up with them.

Also the basic ones used one of those coin cell batteries like the ones used in calculators and the power would get quickly consumed; on the first 1-3 usages the lights would be too intense and you would get woken up startled and annoyed, then the next 3 usages would be perfect for achieving Lucid Dreaming or Astral Projection but then the next time the intensity would be too low to cause any effect because of the low battery. Among these cheap masks there were many DIY projects you could make for less than $30 (Google DIY dream mask).

There is also the problem of building up resistance. To begin with, not everyone experiences Theta state REM 45 – 60 minutes after going to bed. In addition, sometimes the body might avoid going to sleep for the first 45 – 60 minutes to avoid being woken up abruptly by the mask. To counteract this, programmable masks were created in which you could set a timer, flashing intervals, duration, etc.

Then came the real deal; masks that could detect REM through infrared sensors and activate the flashing lights. The best one out there was the Novadreamer which was programmable and also had sound settings, this was definitely cutting edge technology making it the top product back then. Lately I've had the opportunity to see the product and realize that it uses a huge enclosure on the mask plus two AAA batteries which would probably render it very uncomfortable to sleep with, and people said it had many 'false activations' such as moving your head at night would activate the flashing, also it sold close to $1000 initially. The company is currently working on a Novadreamer 2 which will probably solve this problem and incorporate new technology.

Then another mask was released to the market called the 'REM-Dreamer', this mask currently sells for $200, it has a coin cell battery making it way more comfortable than the old Novadreamer and users say it has a high success rate with better REM detection infrared sensors and technology. I also believe the REM Dreamer uses LED lights and constant intensity not depending on battery life.

Keep in mind that these masks are not magic pills, they still need adjusting and require time and effort from the user to work, not everyone has results with them, but reading this book and practicing the techniques can boost your success rate, I know that with my current OBE skill if I would wear these kinds of masks I would get OBEs every night.

The future of dream masks

Because of renewed interest in OBEs lately, new masks are being developed, many of them have become possible through crowdfunding in sites such as Kickstarter.com. The one that is currently being sold in the market is called 'Remee' . It is being marketed as the world's first comfortable and affordable - yet fully functional - lucid dream mask. The best attribute to this mask is its comfort, it is exactly like a regular sleep mask which would make it comfortable enough to sleep with daily. It is also highly programmable and this can be done through their website. The mask uses real LEDs as opposed to the old Christmas tree light diodes. Hopefully this and the new programming capabilities can counteract the intensity problems that old masks had in which the intensity depended on the life of the battery (according to these guys the battery lasts 5-6 months) which is a coin cell battery. This mask cells for $100 making it the cheapest commercially available mask, however, it does not have infrared REM sensor capabilities, thus making it affordable but not 'NEXT GEN'. The best reviews so far continue to favor the REM Dreamer.

OUT OF BODY EXPERIENCES

Other masks currently in development are NeuroOn and Aurora which had very successful Kickstarter crowdfunding campaigns, however, they haven't been released yet, they promise better REM detecting capabilities, comfort and affordability, I have been following their updates, and frankly, I think they are still behind the REM Dreamer in terms of comfort and functionality. We can only wait to see what the future will bring, or at least if prices will go down.

Apps

I downloaded an app from the App Store into my iPhone called "Lucid Dreamer", it was free and easy to use. In reality, it is very similar to an alarm clock, except that it produces soft music (might be binaural too) and turns the screen on an off in order to induce a mild state of alertness without fully waking you up. This happens many times at night during different intervals (I setup mine to start after 56 minutes of going to bed), and then it continues doing its thing all night (I don't know if it does it every 56 minutes or what). The purpose of the app is to take you away from deep dreaming when you're completely unconscious, and put you in a Theta state to achieve an OBE.

I have to say it was so simple that I was skeptical it would work. To my surprise, it made me go lucid in my dream, so I did my thing (induced an OBE), and the next morning when I woke up--I was so happy since it had been a while since the last time I had an astral travel experience, and then I remembered I had set up the Lucid Dreamer and was really pleased to see that it worked the first time. Remember though that I'm an expert OBEer--and it could work at once for you or it could take some time.

You should setup the Lucid Dreamer to start after a specific period of time has passed in which you think you'll be completely asleep.

I saw other similar applications, some of them free, some of them have to be bought but I haven't tried them, just use the keywords 'Lucid Dream'.

Chapter 8: The Magical Technique of the Angel's Trumpet

I hope you're ready for a super interesting OBE technique, as this one involves real elemental magic. Elementals, also known as 'Elementals of Nature' refer to the souls of animals, plants and minerals. I don't know if they are technically the souls but I know they're basically astral bodies of animals, plants and minerals which have a higher intelligence, different manifestations and work hand in hand with nature. Although they're highly intelligent, they're also absolutely naive like small children.

It is said that gnomes and fairies are elementals of nature, they can be perceived differently by each person, and they inspired fables and tales. Children, having their pineal gland not yet atrophied can sometimes see them, which is why children stare with eyes fixed at things we can't see or have 'imaginary friends'. People who have worked on the field or with nature their whole life also seem to be able to perceive them at times; they tell you stories of the time they saw a man running in the field and suddenly disappearing on a rock and how a few days later they would see the same man coming out of the rock in order to disappear again somewhere. It is no secret that cultures such as Native Americans have very strong bonds with nature, develop relationships with elementals, and becomes shamans and wizards of nature.

Humans go through a period of evolution in the physical realm in which we begin our physical existence as minerals, then through thousands of lives we evolve into plants, then animals and then we reach our human existence. Before reaching the human stage, the elemental of nature that we carry in our previous forms seems to have a somehow symbiotic yet independent existence in the astral world, yet once we reach the human stage then this elemental fuses with our different bodies

OUT OF BODY EXPERIENCES

of existence, becoming part of our DNA and carrying all the information from nature in order to help us in the most difficult journey which is human evolution. Then our mind takes the reins of our different bodies and our astral body acts like a vehicle rather than independent from us and awaits for our command every time we go to sleep.

In this fusion, we can still call upon our very own evolved elemental of nature and ask it to intercede for us and communicate with other elementals of nature in order to produce magic and develop relationships with other elementals. This is something that people from many cultures frequently used in the past and modern groups such wiccans and Gnostics still use.

For this magic it is necessary to have an Angel's Trumpet tree (Brugmansia). These trees are popular in the southern USA and are very attractive having big trumpet-like flowers of yellow, orange, or white coloration.

One must take care for the tree, water it often and establish a relationship with it, talk to it, caress its flowers and trunk and once a relationship is established. then one can sit next to it and say the following call:

"Dear father, you who are my true being, my interior God, I ask you to please command my elemental intercessor to communicate with the elemental of this Angel's Trumpet tree , and ask for its assistance in order to help me to have an Astral Travel when going to bed. Dear Angel's Trumpet please help me, I beseech thee, KAAAAAAAAAMMMMM, KAAAAAAAAAMMMMM, KAAAAAAAAAMMMMM."

Then take one dried flower from the tree and put it under your pillow, then use this new Mantram: Inhale

KAAAAAAAAAMMMMM,

Inhale

KAAAAAAAAAMMMMM, etc. which can also be done mentally by following the tips previously discussed in the book.

There's a twist though, in this occasion you're going to get direct help from the elemental of the Angel's trumpet who will show up in the Astral. The elemental can look like a human boy but it can also take similar shapes. In my case, it appeared as some sort of pubescent tree boy if that makes any sense, basically a tree with legs and arms and facial features. Therefore, it is important to be relaxed and have no fear.

The elemental gave me a hand when in sleep paralysis in order to pull my out of my physical body. It was such a weird sensation to see this talking tree boy in front of me and I told him I needed him to help me out of my body every night whenever he could. I asked for his name and he said his name was "Joaka". His personality was like a puppy, completely innocent.

We went downstairs in the astral dimension's version of the house I was living in and we paid a visit to my little reef tank I had in the kitchen. I had been having problems with the corals that were looking in a poorer state everyday even though I kept measuring the parameters and taking tests and everything was perfect. I asked Joaka if he could communicate with the corals and tell me what was wrong with them. Joaka for some reason was suddenly absent and I heard the corals whispering in a very sharp voice, I got closer and I could clearly hear what they were saying: "The light, the light, it is too strong!"

At the end of my journey I said goodbye to my new friend Joaka and promised to take care of him and water him every day. The next morning I started taking some measures such as raising the lamp and getting a dimmable ballast in order to reduce the light intensity.

A few days later my Guru who has his special senses fully awake was in town, he doesn't know anything about reef keeping, and while we were having dinner in the kitchen I asked him if he could communicate with the corals and find out why they were looking so bad. I didn't tell him I had talked to them in the astral a few days ago. He remained in silence for a few seconds, and then said "The light, it is too intense for the coral frags which are still very small. It is good for bigger corals colonies but not for small pieces".

At you can see, communicating with the elementals is very helpful and a wonderful experience, the knowledge than can be obtained can be applied to many different fields. There are thousands of different kinds of elementals one can interact

OUT OF BODY EXPERIENCES

with, all of them look different and have different properties, some of them for instance, are good at healing, they can even heal by the distance, some others such as Aloe plants are excellent for protection against negative forces, and Angels' trumpets are good for having OBEs.

Chapter 9: Your First Steps in the Astral Dimension

I remember during my first OBEs I was exploring the astral dimension with an orb-like field of vision and movement, which of course made navigation more complicated, and I also felt some vertigo from not having a body. This can be solved easily, all you need to do is to use your mind to shape your astral body. Just imagine a translucent body that you can move the same way you do with your physical body, this will make navigation and interaction easier but most people who have an OBE already experience using this translucent body from the very first time, which means that our mind is very used to having a body with a head, two legs and two arms—but I'm just mentioning the orb experience in case you go through it.

One of the coolest things of the astral world is that you can fly! So try this wonderful new experience, it is really fun! Just take a jump and use your imagination to steer and move. If you want to reach your house's roof then just go outside, take a jump and imagine landing on the rooftop. With time you'll be able to fly around cities and at a great speed, it just requires practice.

In case you're feeling heavy and having a difficult time taking off, you can try a simple technique: take a small jump and cross your legs together as if you were sitting in the air, then point your index finger upwards and concentrate on floating and gaining altitude, and you will slowly move upward. If you want to go down just point your finger downwards.

One of the questions I get asked often is: Once I'm in the astral, what should I do?

The possibilities are limitless of course. I would suggest to explore your room surroundings first, try to touch objects and see how they feel. You can also try to get your hand through the wall. At the beginning it will feel like a normal wall, you can even feel the texture, but with a little added pressure your hand will go through it.

OUT OF BODY EXPERIENCES

As I've mentioned before, your physical body may or may not be present. If you notice it's not there, it's not unusual as you are in a higher dimensional space, and it's not supposed to be exactly the same as your physical surroundings If however it is there, be careful of looking at it—as it may pull you back into it.

In fact, staying in the astral dimension is hard--it requires a lot of concentration to not fall into a dream or waking out of it, so try to remain as calm as possible. You could start feeling sleepy and or losing concentration, or your field of vision can start losing clarity--these are all signs that you are about to fall into a dream or wake up, you don't want that. In the astral you must keep your emotions in check, never too excited, never too rushed, never scared, or you will ruin the experience.

The movie "The Matrix" had an interesting analogy to this that I noticed. The people of Zion, the community outside of the Matrix, were all extremely serene and meditative. This is how you need to be when you astral travel.

Keeping yourself grounded to the astral

If you think you're about to fall into a dream or wake up then start touching objects that seem solid in the astral, such as the walls. These will have a similar feeling as in the physical dimension, and they will help to keep you grounded.

Also you can place the palms of your hands together in a praying position and the sole of your feet together as well in a foot-praying position. The palms and feet soles have very powerful vortexes for interacting with the world, placing them together helps you to concentrate and keep yourself in the moment.

Astral Visibility

When exploring the astral you will notice different degrees of clarity, for instance, since most OBEs happen at night time then the astral could look dark, but this is actually a mind thing since in reality the astral does not have night periods. Also, your vision could become blurry which is a sign of losing concentration and waking up/starting to dream.

The more aware you are during your day to day, the clearer and brighter the astral is going to be when you're having your body. In other words, clarity in the astral depends on your general level of conscious awareness.

You can increase your astral visibility/awareness by being in a constant state of attention during the day, not day dreaming or thinking about silly stuff, overthinking things or being worried all of the time. Mindfulness meditation is also highly advisable to increase your awareness since the purpose of meditation is to keep you in the moment, focused and not being carried away by the mind.

Once you're in the astral, the previously mentioned techniques to keep you grounded will help to increase your visibility, light and clarity but there's another really powerful technique to help you with this, just say the following prayer with a lot of faith and focus:

"Divine mother, I beg you to please give me more clarity, give me more light so that I can see better"

The prayer doesn't have to be exactly like that, but must contain the words 'Divine Mother' 'please' and asking for clarity, better vision, light, etc.

You will see then how the astral world begins to light up.

Traveling to places far away

Apart from exploring your room's surroundings, try taking a walk on the street, or attempting an overseas voyage. One of my favorite places to go is Egypt, it is also a place where most people feel a connection to, so my advice is to first get out of your house, and then think about Egypt. You could imagine the pyramids and then ask the following:

"Divine Mother (or father) please take me to Egypt!"

Then take a jump and keep the image of Egypt on your mind.

OUT OF BODY EXPERIENCES

You will now begin to feel a force moving you at high speeds in the air, sometimes you could start being 'sucked up' by the ground which just means that the quickest way to Egypt is a straight line across the earth, or you could just instantly appear in Egypt, which is the way that traveling long distances in the astral is usually done.

If you go through objects or get dizzy, or the speed is so fast that you can't see well and start feeling vertigo, then just remember to relax, keep the image of your destination in your mind and put your palm on your solar plexus (navel). The solar plexus is the center of emotions and covering it with your palm prevents it from absorbing the information that is upsetting you. You can use the command above to travel anywhere you'd like.

My journeys into Egypt

In one of my first astral journeys to Egypt I was able to visit the pyramids and be inside of the Great Pyramid of Cheops. It was dark inside and I was being led through different halls, seeing anthropomorphic statues and animal masks, and the images of Gods and guardians from the past. These types of astral experiences are spiritually important. I was probably being welcomed or having an initiation--then everything went dark and I woke up, though the experience continued in my internal bodies without me consciously realizing it.

In a second astral journey to Egypt, I asked my divine mother to be taken to Egypt again and this time I was taken to an Egyptian museum. I walked through--it staring at the priceless archeological pieces. I remembered that the museum had a lot of balustrades of a particular classic style. When I woke up, I immediately Googled 'Egyptian Museum' and I found images of Cairo's museum which was the exact same museum I visited in the astral, and many of the pictures actually showed the same balustrades which served as a proof that I really visited Cairo's museum. A few months ago before finishing this book I had the opportunity to finally visit the museum in the physical and it was incredible to see many of the pieces I saw in the astral!

KENSHO

Finally, the third time I visited Egypt in the astral was actually because asked to see Atlantis. I was taken to the Great Sphinx and took an underground entrance on the right paw of the Sphinx. There was a tunnel made of bricks, it looked like a chimney made of sand-colored bricks, and I could not see the bottom. It was dark and I began descending--floating down the dark tunnel. Although oddly, there seemed to be some torches placed within. Then I finally reached a room which was full of golden figures and artifacts. I could not understand what these artifacts were but pretty much everything seemed to be made of gold. I also saw plates with golden figures as if they sculpted them out of gold instead of using paints. This was interesting because later on I read somewhere that Atlanteans didn't get to fully incorporate painting as a means of artistic expression, so instead they used paintings only to paint their houses--which correlates with the type of art that I saw.

Since my experience I've read many stories that talk about the hidden room under the right paw of the Sphinx, many new age authors, particularly Edgar Cayce, describe it as "A Hall of Records" containing all the wisdom of the lost civilization of Atlantis and the true history of the human race. Some of these authors actually say these artifacts were rescued from Atlantis before it sank. This is incredible since it all relates to my experience and I believe many of these stories probably came from people who were able to have OBEs and go to this places just like me!

Archeologists have also excavated under the right paw of the Sphinx trying to find these treasures and found a system of corridors and rooms that were empty. The easiest explanation is that these treasures had been looted...However, some authors say that these treasures remain safe in the 4th dimension. I believe this is the case because when I physically visited Egypt recently I had the opportunity of being inside the Great Pyramid of Cheops and do a practice inside with the help of my Guru.

Within the Great Pyramid is the so-called King's Chamber, which was found empty by archeologists. Inside there's a stone coffin or casket that allegedly could have contained Cheops' remains, however the coffin seemed to be finished in a rush with

OUT OF BODY EXPERIENCES

not much detail, and the same can be said about the chamber which has no detail at all, something that is contrary to the other tombs of Pharaoh's found in Egypt. So, why would a Pharaoh invest so much effort, years and details creating the Great Sphinx and leave his chamber and coffin with no decoration or inscription at all?

According to my Guru, the place is full of treasures and Cheops' real mummy and coffin are in the 4th dimension, but the bare chamber is all that we get to see in the 3rd dimension. This is part of the magic of ancient Egypt, so I believe the same happens with the chambers under the Sphinx which seemed to be empty.

Creating stuff in the astral.

This is a really cool way to see the law of attraction in action (thoughts become reality). Once you're having an OBE simply imagine something you want to appear. I like to imagine that I can shoot energy balls from my hands so I stare at my right palm and imagine an energy ball forming up and it does!

Then you can practice changing the color of the energy ball to green, red, orange, blue, purple, whatever you want. This is a good exercise for your creativity. Then you can try to create other things like swords, shields, cars, etc. If you can think it you can create it in the astral. The better your imagination is the faster things will be created. In the physical the same principles apply but since there are more laws then things don't happen instantly nor do they simply appear: they have to go through lengthy processes which require many steps and situations to happen, such as avoiding negative interference and actively participating through physical work, collaborations, etc. in other words, thoughts must first pass through more laws, time and mental energy to be crystalized in the physical. In the Astral world, present, past and future happen at the same time, which is why thoughts manifest instantly. This is due to the Astral having 12 laws while the physical world has 48. Recall how fewer laws mean happier beings, and the more laws there are the more complication and the more suffering that can occur.

Chapter 10: Lucid Dreaming Techniques

As we discussed earlier, Lucid Dreaming is to 'wake up in a dream' or become aware of dreaming. This is also great since we can either explore our dream world and interact and gather information from our subconscious mind or, with practice, eliminate the dream scenery created by the mind and interact with the purest Astral World.

The movie 'Inception' a recent Hollywood hit directed by Christopher Nolan talks about lucid dreaming: in the movie, a crew uses some sort of technology to induce collective lucid dreaming in order to "seed" ideas in a person's mind, interacting with the person's dream world while being aware.

Like in the movie, interacting with your dreams can be fascinating: you can find the answers about yourself and how your mind works, and you can also use the subjective dream world as a gateway into the objective astral world.

Practicing astral projection techniques can trigger lucid dreaming, too. For instance, when a dream mask activates, you may become aware of your surroundings in the dream world, and then choose to explore the dream world instead of choosing to go out of your body.

Most lucid dreaming techniques are based on "reality checks": these are done during the day and are repeated in a dream.

Finger Pulling

This reality check consists on pulling your index finder (pull it hard but don't hurt yourself) and asking yourself whether you're in the physical or in a lucid dream. You do this many times a day, in fact, it is a constant reminder. You can do this anywhere without anyone noticing, the question can be done mentally. You

OUT OF BODY EXPERIENCES

should always give the answer, now here's the interesting part; if you repeatedly do this technique during the day then you will automatically remember to do it while dreaming and when you do, if you pull hard enough and the finger will stretch like bubble gum! Since this is a very unusual dream trait, then the answer will be "I'm dreaming" and at that moment you will gain instant awareness.

Jumping

This is another reality check similar to finger pulling. You simply ask yourself whether you're in the physical or in the dream world and take a little jump. If you do this in the dream then you will start floating and you will know for sure that you're dreaming. The only inconvenience with this technique is that it is harder to not be noticed by other people when done in public but it is a powerful reality check.

Totems

In the movie Inception, when a person found themselves in a dream, they could pull out their totem in order to know if they were in their own dream or another's. In this case, a totem was a special object that had something off about it which only they could identify.

For instance, common pocket-carrying –sized objects that were lighter than normal, such as a specially carved dice. Since the technology is not there yet, it is unlikely that we will find ourselves in somebody else's dream, but we can still use totems as reality checks to know if we're dreaming.

You want to choose a small object you can keep with you at all times. Throughout the day, whenever you see or touch this object, do a reality check. Then, in your dreams, you're likely to pull out that item and use it for a reality check. Chances are likely that in your dream, the totem will have different or strange writing or shapes on it rather than what you know is actually there, and this can trigger your awareness to make you realize you're dreaming.

Evacuation

When I was a kid I used to have many nightmares caused by looking at the monsters from the covers of horror videotapes, as well as TV trailers. In my dreams I would be chased by these monsters and wake up covered in sweat and terrified. There was a particular monster that would often appear in my dreams and freak me out. So I created a technique to wake me up from dreaming (you may recall I talked about this at the beginning of the book, and how I used this technique to later enable OBEs). When I started feeling scared in a dream that was turning into a nightmare, I would open my eyelids in the dream as wide as possible, which would actually cause my physical eyelids to open and this would swiftly wake me up from the nightmare in a state of alertness, and then when in my room I would stand up to turn on the lights and try to keep myself from falling asleep until I was sure I was awake and not in the nightmare.

Once you have done a reality check and know you are dreaming then open your eyelids in the dream as wide as possible and this will wake you up. You must learn with practice to control it as to not wake you up swiftly and alerted but rather softly enough to be taken out of the dream and getting a quick glimpse of your room but still feeling sleepy as opposed to alert and sweaty. If done right then you will find yourself in your room with sleep paralysis, and you can then try the detaching techniques to have an OBE. When I started experimenting with lucid dreaming masks, I would try this technique once the lights were flashing in the dream, and it was always with great results.

Inception

We'll define this as 'seeding' ideas or commands into your mind so that you can have changes in your personality, attitudes and life in general. This is possible while Lucid Dreaming and it is related to self-hypnotism but the experience is more powerful because not only you get to seed ideas into your mind but you

OUT OF BODY EXPERIENCES

can also get answers right away through direct messages, symbols, or images.

One way to do it is that once you start having a lucid dream and are conscious, you sit down and say the following phrase three times: "Let my mind record this command in my memory, permanently and at all times and do everything to fulfill it".

You then say the command three times, ex. "I want to have more confidence"

And finally you say "Let this command be fulfilled", three times.

The command must be simple and positive, never use a negative such as "I don't want to suffer", instead you could say, "I want to be happy", "I want to be happier", etc.

Another way to do Inception is to interact with "dream characters". Most of the people you'll see while lucid dreaming are not real people, nor the astral body of people (well, some of them are but we'll discuss that in another chapter), but are rather creations of your own mind, therefore, they're connected to your mind on many levels (conscious, subconscious, infraconscious, super conscious). You can interrogate or give commands to these characters as a method of communicating to all aspects of your being.

Don't ask them questions about themselves because they won't know how to answer, they're just illusions and they'll just get stuck there wasting your time. Instead, ask them questions about yourself and they will answer in a direct or symbolic language. You can also give them commands such as we learned above and the way to do it would be, for example: "I want to be more outgoing", "tell my mind to become more confident", "we need to be more positive in order to work better" etc. They are there for you but they need your instructions, commands and discipline (something they are not used to).

Over time you'll be transformed into a better person.

From Lucid to Pure Astral

By having a Lucid Dream, you're already in the Astral World, the Fifth Dimension, but since you just 'woke up' in a dream then your vision is still blurred with dream scenery and characters that, if not careful, will make you fall asleep again and lose consciousness.

Therefore, the best strategy is to ignore all the current scenery and characters and start focusing on what you want to do and where you want to go, then the dream scenery and characters will disappear and you will see the Astral in its pure form.

You can also use the Divine Mother prayer to assist you in removing the mind's illusions.

"Divine mother, I beg you to please give me more clarity, give me more light so that I can see better, please take away all the dream and let me see the pure Astral World"

Chapter 11: Meeting People While Out of Body

There are five types of people you'll meet while OBEing: Mind Creations, Enlightened Beings, Other OBErs from the Physical World, Temporal Astral Residents, and Permanent Astral Residents. How can one tell apart between them?

Mind Creations

Mind creations are the more common occurrences. The astral world including, of course, dreams are full of them. They represent thoughts you had during the day, as well as programs and egos, new and old, everything you carry in your mind, which are all part of your inner-mental world.

One can easily find out that they're mental creations by asking them questions about themselves, for instance, you can ask them what their name is and most times they will not know how to answer and remain mute with a blank stare, same thing would happen if they are asked 'what do you do for a living?'.

In the astral, one can observe that these mind creations have a short programming, they might engage in repeating stuff you did during the day, ask you questions or try to do simple interactions that lead nowhere such as asking 'where's the store?'. Most of them will be seen when dreaming and gaining lucidity (lucid dreaming). The more aware a person is, the less the astral will have these mind creations during that particular OBE. If the person is having a direct Astral Projection instead of Lucid Dreaming then these mind creations will be scarce but if the person starts losing awareness during a particular projection session, then the mind creations will become more common, until the projector is dreaming again.

These mind creations can also be your mind's stereotypical representation of someone you know in the physical: For example, I had a friend who suffered from

KENSHO

advanced bipolarity. One day I was having a dream and suddenly acquired lucidity, then I saw this bipolar friend running at me and yelling like crazy, like a true madman. In the real life he's of course not that extreme, but I do refer at him as a crazy guy often, and perhaps this running crazy image was his stereotypical representation that I created in my mind.

Seeing people running at you and screaming in the astral can startle you, but I was aware enough in this session in order to be calm and feel unthreatened, this is a good thing because should I have acted scared of him and ducked for cover, but then he could have attacked me since my fears would have given that specific programming to this mental representation. So, instead since I stood there calm, he didn't know what to do once he was an inch in front of me, and for some weird reason it just occurred to me to put my finger through his forehead like the T1000 in that famous Terminator 2 scene, and I told him 'you're not real, just disappear' and he started shaking, collapsed and disappeared. That worked so well that I started doing it more often with other dream images that would get in my way.

Like I said, he could have attacked me should I have shown fear, which demonstrated that mind creations can get programmed by my fears and emotions, so that taught me that I could program them to do beneficial things instead, such as changing my mindset. As what I discussed before as inception; I could program them to give me more confidence, to give me more happiness, etc. After all, they were the stuff that I had in my mind, so why not fill my mind with positive and useful commands?

I soon discovered, they were actually a direct link to my mind, to the superconscious, and also to the infra-conscious mind, and even though they had very little programming about themselves, they seemed to know everything about me and sometimes they could even be a link to my higher self.

I would tell them I needed to communicate with my mind about an issue I was having and asked for possible courses of action or ask them questions about myself and they would answer; sometimes in direct language, sometimes in dream language, sometimes with a visual representation that would be

OUT OF BODY EXPERIENCES

logical or illogical (surreal). I also found out that I could summon my Divine Father or Divine Mother through them as well. I'm sure that the father of analytical psychology, Carl Gustav Jung also had similar interactions with his mind through lucid dreams and OBEs, I've read some of his work on dream interpretation and archetypes, though I've never finished any of his books I'm sure he talks about similar conclusions.

Enlightened Beings

Enlightened beings can be met in the astral, but they usually only appear when they have an important message to give you or when they see that you're having spiritual progress and decide to guide you. These beings can appear as masters, saints, gods and archetypes.

The easiest to find which can also be called upon (through invocation) are the Divine Mother and Divine Father. They represent the Divine Feminine and Divine Masculine archetypes of your soul, they are a part of your internal God and care for your spiritual evolution.

The Divine Mother is the easiest to call upon, she's the one that spoils you sometimes, easiest to talk to, more flexible, sweet and caring. The Divine Father is more strict an demanding and requires certain merits to be called upon. They will show you things, they will give you the knowledge and the answers you're looking for, sometimes in a direct language though mostly symbolic, they can also take you to places, teach you things and introduce you to other enlightened beings.

The invocation for the Divine Father or Divine Mother is the following:

AANNTIIIAAA DAUNA SASTAZAAAAAA!!!!! (The 'TIII' part sounds like Tea)

Divine mother (**or father**) please come here! (say this 3 times)

KENSHO

By the power of the light! (Say this 3 times)

Repeat from the beginning until the Divine Mother or Father shows up.

Always be respectful when addressing them and always say 'please'.

I have done some experiments in which I direct myself to a mind creation in the form of a person such as a woman, for example, and I ask her to bring the Divine Mother, or I do the invocation in front of her and she suddenly changes into the Divine Mother. Your intuition in the astral or in a lucid dream is stronger, and you feel like the person you're talking to is not a mind creation anymore but something more powerful. The same applies to the Divine Father if you do the same with a Mind Creation of a man.

I've received many teachings from different Masters in the astral, and some experiences can be life changing such as when I met Paramahansa Yogananda and he allowed me to see the immortal Babaji. I felt an indescribable bliss as well as enormous energy, so much that it woke me up but the image got imprinted in my memory.

OBErs from the Physical

Believe it or not, it is hard to discern between mind creations and real people. The astral dimension works in many ways that are different than the physical dimension and for this reason some people who are dreaming are transported to spaces in the astral in which they interact with the projections of their mind (dreaming) while remaining invisible to other people in the astral. At times a person who's aware in the astral can see them; especially when they are people living in the same house, as the house itself has a powerful grounding energy. For instance, I've seen my parents in the astral on a few occasions.

The main problem with real people in the astral is that they remain dreaming. In case you were ever curious what you look like objectively as you dream, this is a good opportunity to

OUT OF BODY EXPERIENCES

see for yourself. You'll encounter people who look just like themselves; with their same clothes, but when talking to them you can see that they're staring at nothing since they're following the images they have in their mind instead of being aware of the astral dimension. Sometimes, their mind projections can even be seen by the astral traveler, as well. When you speak to them, they will hardly listen or understand you and they will answer by mumbling, it is very similar to what happens when trying to interact with sleep-walkers in the physical.

Sometimes they can be awakened in the astral if you tell them they're dreaming but this is not recommended since it is very hard to do so and even if it works, if the person is not familiar with having OBEs then most likely they will only be conscious for a few seconds—just to lose consciousness again and forget everything the next day.

Only try this with other fellow astral travelers who are familiar with the astral or who really want to do it. Remember that time is precious, and if you waste all of your energy on trying to make contact with a sleeping person, you may end up waking up and wasting your experience.

Now, you can also meet other fellow astral travelers who are aware in the astral. With practice you will realize it is very uncommon to see them, most of the times they will be mental creations of your friends and family. The way to discern it is when they engage you and have more lines and interaction that makes more sense. Intuition also plays a role and if they were real people you knew then they will remember meeting you in the astral the next day. It seems sometimes there's a connection that can make practitioners meet in the astral no matter the distance.

A story of how I met a co-worker in the astral

One night I was in the Astral just flying all over the city and enjoying myself when I passed on top of a roundabout and I heard somebody calling me. I looked down and I saw a girl my age calling 'over here!'. I landed with caution as I thought this could possibly be another mind creation (like I said, meeting people who are conscious in the astral is rare) and she began talking to me. She invited me to her house which was right next to the roundabout and a public telephone, and once we entered her room her conversation was focused on her problems being single and feeling lonely in life. All this time I was unsure she was real so I just listened but didn't tell her much, I remember I spent quite a while talking to her in the astral until I woke up.

Two months later I landed a job in a candy factory and I was introduced to my only co-worker. After greeting her she told me 'Do you know anything about OBEs?', 'Yes I have them all the time, why?', 'Because I remember I met you in the Astral'. Then I mentioned the episode of the roundabout and the house and the conversation and she said 'Yes it was my house'. I was amazed, it was the first time that I had met somebody in the astral who I then met in the physical. On another day she invited me to her house and it was exactly the same house I had seen in the astral; with the roundabout and the public telephone. This totally contradicts the scientist's explanations on the OBE phenomena in which they basically say that everything is just imagination and confused senses.

Other than my co-worker, I have to admit that I haven't met many other people who were aware in the astral; except for my Guru whom I met several times and who can perfectly describe when I talk to him the next day about our interaction in the Astral and the teachings he taught me.

I remember one day I had an OBE while staying in my Guru's house and I went straight to the living room where I found a group of people wearing white coats and doing scientific experiments; they had a TV and what appeared to be motion capture devices, which they appeared to be using for motion detection experiments similar to the technology on the XBOX 360 Kinect. All the equipment I was seeing looked very real, just like in the physical, except that the scientists didn't seem to realize they were in the astral; they were probably just repeating the stuff they do in their day to day. They were even showing me how the whole thing worked and were very enthusiastic.

Then I saw my guru at the door and he was wearing a cap he sometimes wears in the physical and he looked at me

OUT OF BODY EXPERIENCES

cautiously to see if I was aware or not and said 'What's up?'. I told him 'Master who are these people?', 'oh they're some scientists who I'm helping with some experiments to develop new technologies', 'Oh OK', 'I have to take care of some business so why don't you seat yourself and see them working?".

I sat down and saw them working, but it was taking them some time and I got bored and decided to leave by flying through the hall and left the house to go for a flight.

The next day in the morning I saw my guru in the physical wearing the same cap and told me 'Hello, what's up?' with the same inquisitive stare, wanting to know if I remember what happened the night before. 'Master, you were with a group of scientists doing some experiments right?'. He laughed and nodded.

'So what was that they were doing?', 'I'm helping them with motion detection technology, in the future there will be no buttons and everything will be motion detection', he went on explaining that he was creating inceptions in their dreams in order to boost technological advances for the progress of mankind. It was not the first time that he had done this, as he had helped people from different areas, even musicians and movie directors. This is why sometimes Hollywood films such as 'The Matrix' seem to have some deep ideas on spiritual life and existentialism. He's of course not the only Master helping with incepting ideas in the mind of people, as there are many Masters who are helping mankind in different areas. They always target somebody who has some power or creative influence in the world and who can deliver something to the masses. They can also do the same in the minds of politicians in order to avoid or delay wars. Of course, there are some rules about how they go about these actions, but the methods they use are perfectly valid according to the law of Karma.

Temporary Astral Residents

It is also possible to meet temporary astral residents These are people who lived in the third dimension not long ago and now they live in the 5th dimension, in other words, many of them will be our dead relatives (we say "temporary" because most in the astral who came from the 3rd dimension are sorting out their karma and waiting to eventually return to the physical world). A real person can also be difficult to tell apart from, once again, those pesky mind creations. Dead relatives however present themselves when they want to share an important message, or especially when they had recently passed away, and by applying some discernment skills you can tell if it was real or not.

They are more frequently encountered when they have just passed away, and the astral traveler simply 'runs into' them and that means the dead relative wanted to say goodbye or share something for the benefit of the live relative. Another situation is the dead relative might need help in order to lose a burden that is hindering their advancement in the afterlife; and request the live relative to solve some unfinished business for the dead person. This timing, the nature of the conversation as well as the OBEr's intuition is what allows one to realize whether a dead relative was encountered or if it was a mind creation.

When people die, many times they carry the same pains and thoughts they had before passing away without realizing they are in the astral. It's as if they're dreaming, and the degree of awareness they can have in the astral greatly depends on their Karma which is also related to the awareness they had during life; if the person was mostly good and had a righteous life, then those positive life decisions are linked to greater awareness. It doesn't take much time for such individuals to realize they had passed away and start enjoying their lives in the astral world in a positive way in which this higher dimension can be like a heaven to them. They will live happily in this dimension until eventually it is the right time for them to go back and be born again. This can happen in a week or it can take many decades--it all depends on the person's karma.

Also, depending on his karma, the person can make certain choices as to where and how to be born again. This option happens to people who made good deeds in life, who were mostly upright and especially to those who strived on working on their spiritual progress. What choices would they

OUT OF BODY EXPERIENCES

have available? Their Divine Mother most likely would walk the person through it and show him the possibilities:

"You can be born in this rich family, everything would be given to you but there's the chance that you will never feel truly happy as a grownup and you would stray from the spiritual path. Or, there's this other family, they don't have that much money but there will be always bread on the table. They are artists, they can teach you beautiful talents that will be useful for your adult life... Now, there's this other family--they're poor, your father will abandon you and you will be hungry in your childhood, but to make up for it we'll give you a strong will, endurance, and the ability to lead others and a drive to accomplish great things and guide mankind, and your reward will be the greatest of all." These are just examples of the choices given to a person who is about to be re-born again.

I have flashbacks of when I was in the astral plane and ready to be born again. It seemed as if at one point I stopped being an old person who had recently passed away and started becoming younger again, until I became like an astral kid and I had my beautiful Divine Mother who guided me (I still do). She was incredibly compassionate and sweet with me, and she would show me the family I was going to be born in. As I'm writing this I'm also getting flashbacks of my father, but most of all I remember my mother sitting in a sofa gently caressing her belly with a big smile in her face absolutely happy for the baby that was going to be born in a few months, such an incredible warm peaceful feeling. I could feel a love beyond description and a natural bond with this my mother to be. I remembered I would cry to my Divine Mother that I was so eager to meet my physical mother that I wanted to be born now and be held in her arms. "Soon", my divine mother would reply.

Finally when the day to be born arrived, it felt as if going down on a rollercoaster. I tried to hold on to anything so as not to be sucked out of the astral--such vertigo! And I remember my divine mother comforting me to let go until I finally fell down the rollercoaster and was received in shock, and with a spank on my butt, then I was held in my mother's arm and it made it all better.

I don't remember having other choices to be born in, perhaps I did and don't remember, but it is obvious to me that I must have been a good person because I was born in a wonderful family. It would seem the greater part of mankind is not that lucky.

It is said that the divine beings give us "the cup of forgetfulness" before being born again so that we can better live our new lives and better enjoy our freewill. I don't know if that's just an allegory or we actually forget from the passing of time and the shock of being born.

Children have clearer memories of their life in the astral dimension, but they too forget with time. My Guru remembers every single life he's had but it is not clear to me if he was born knowing or he acquired these memories when he became a Master. My intuition tells me that once a person has awakened for good; when that person has become enlightened and liberated then it is as if that person realizes that he never forgot what he was, always has been, and will always be.

Permanent Residents of the Astral

Do we always have to come back? For most beings the answer is yes, we cannot stop the cycle of being reborn until we pay all of our karma, which normally happens when the person has acquired sufficient spiritual progress in order to eliminate his/her egos and "I"'s. And once these attachments are removed then the person is no longer bound to the physical world, and can continue his evolutionary path in the astral where he/she will have other missions, other works to do, other learning to receive and other types of lives to master. These are what we would call the Permanent Residents of the Astral World: People who once lived on earth or other planets and were able to liberate themselves from the chains of the physical dimension. These beings are completely aware in the Astral World, and thus they have the ability to create at will in the physical. They create beautiful places, castles, temples, and they fill the Astral Dimension with all sorts of beautiful manifestations of architecture, music, painting, the arts, etc. And they interact with

OUT OF BODY EXPERIENCES

yet more advanced beings such as Divine Archetypes, Angels, Gods, and Masters (Avatars).

The astral world has countries too, with magnificent temples that can be visited where Masters give teachings to the Astral residents. Some of these temples include the Temple of Chapultepec, the Temple of Alden, and the Temple of Montsalvat--just to name a few that I know of.

These astral residents can also have missions to perform for the benefit of people in the 3rd dimension, influencing us from the astral world. And once they have achieved their evolution in the astral plane then they will be able to live in yet higher planes.

It is for this reason that the will for liberation and spiritual progress should be present in all of us. I highly recommend to practice meditation in your life in order to gain awareness which will lead you to a quest for further spiritual knowledge and progress.

Setting up a collective practice

If you have friends who are also OBE practitioners and want to meet in the astral, it is doable. To accomplish this, you must think about the person you want to meet in the astral, and you will be automatically taken to where that person is as long as that person is also aware at that moment in the astral. However, in practice it is really hard for different factors. Namely, not everybody has the sufficient skill to OBE every night, also, if they are able to OBE most likely everyone will have a different time to do so, because while everyone can agree at a specific time, unfortunately these things don't work by the clock.

For this reason, special collective practices can be arranged to improve the chances of meeting in the astral. The way to do it is to meet at somebody's house or practice center and bring bunk beds or sleeping bags and mats. You want these improvised beds to not be as comfortable as your normal bed, and use them exclusively for your OBE practices.

Then everyone goes to sleep at the same time in the facing up position and using the same technique, in this case it is

KENSHO

recommended to use a mantram technique verbally and then proceed mentally.

Once in the astral you can meet the other practitioners who also had the OBE, or sometimes you will be able to see their astral bodies dreaming, in which case it is completely valid to grab their hands and try to pull them out, or talk them into waking up in the astral. This is the only time in which I recommend the latter, since any other time it is a waste of time-- but in this occasion there's predisposition to make it work.

If you're going for the collective practice, it is also recommended to have a light dinner and to do meditation practices before going to sleep, as this will empower the practice a lot.

OUT OF BODY EXPERIENCES

Chapter 12: Final Words

This is the conclusion to this book. The knowledge that we've provided in it is sufficient to have the best results and increase your chances. However, it will require lots of practice, a positive attitude and constant dedication to achieve it. These methods should become a routine to be practiced every night. A year has 365 days which means 365 times to put the techniques to practice, which is quite a lot in order to achieve at least one experience.

It is of paramount importance to do practices to strengthen one's awareness; practices such as meditation and being in the moment. You must avoid daydreaming and being carried away by your egos and emotions. Practice meditation, practice, practice.

The amount of knowledge that one can get from the Astral has no limits and it will help you to open your mind, your creativity, your understanding of life and death and the purpose of life, but as if it wasn't enough already, we're currently in the process of writing a follow up book with advanced practices. This follow up book will contain information about:

- Seeing past existences
- Visiting healing temples to heal oneself and others remotely
- Visiting planet Venus
- Journeying into the Akashic Records, where all the information of mankind is stored, (and can be visualized, i.e., seeing what the Atlantean culture was like)
- Other Astral Magic techniques
- Visiting the Temple of Universal Language (to learn languages), as well as visiting other temples.
- Techniques to visit the fourth dimension with your physical body! (Another physical superior dimension where the Mayans and other cultures still exist, with other dimensional laws such as different time.
- And more.

77

Currently, one of the most valuable places to continue your journey and share thoughts with myself and others is the Facebook group I have created. We check this group daily and give answers and comments in order to improve your practices and to further the goal of creating a community of OBErs. To get involved, please follow this link on your Facebook account:

My best wishes and may the light guide you in your journey!

About the Author

Kensho had an ordinary life in the way most people would call ordinary; he had a career in business administration and a job from 8 to 5. Yet, he was bored with a standard that wasn't providing real fulfillment.

Ever since he was a kid, he had had spiritual interests, always wanting to understand what the meaning of life was. When he was in his teenage years, he began having uncontrolled out of body experiences that he couldn't understand, and that's when he began studying Gnosis and received practical knowledge to control these experiences and get the most out of

KENSHO

them. In this moment he began to find the answers he was looking for.

In 2010 he met his Guru, Dharmapa Rimpoché. He quit his job and moved to the foothills of a small town in Guanajuato, Mexico, to study with his Guru to become a Zen Buddhist missionary for the Prajna Movement.

In 2011 he opened a meditation center in Zamora, Mexico. In this year he was admitted as a student in the Order of the Yellow Dragon and received his Dharma name Kensho, which means "Clear Vision" in Japanese.

Then in 2012, he moved to San Diego, California to help establish the Prajna Meditation Center in El Cajon which is still open today. In San Diego he became familiar with the teachings of Yogananda and Babaji.

Kensho walks the middle path; which is a type of a spiritual path about living life to the fullest among normal people, doing the daily required chores, and providing service to others.

Kensho's knowledge comes from the teachings of his guru Zen Buddhist Master Dharmapa Rimpoché, and Gnostic Master Samael Aun Weor, as well as his life experiences and anecdotes.

At some point he thought about becoming a celibate monk, but he realized he was too handsome for that.

He currently lives in-Prague, Czech Republic.

More By Developed Life Books

You can find more books at the following address: www.developedlife.com/bookstore. You can also head to www.developedlife.com/kensho to continue your education in out of body experiences.

Until next time!

Copyright 2015: Cyrus Kirkpatrick, Developed Life Books, C.K. Media Enterprises L.L.C., All Rights Reserved

KENSHO

NOTES PAGES
(Please journal in the following pages your important
discoveries and experiences as you practice the art of leaving
your body.)

OUT OF BODY EXPERIENCES

KENSHO

Printed in Great Britain
by Amazon